The Painful Harassment or School Bullying

By Milagros Santiago Irizarry

Translated from Spanish by Joni Radcliff
& José Alejandro Peña

Obsidiana Press

The Painful Harassment or School Bullying

Milagros Santiago Irizarry

Translated from Spanish by Joni Radcliff
& José Alejandro Peña

Obsidiana Press
www.obsidianapress.com

ISBN 978-1-960434-23-4

© Cover photograph by Milagros Santiago Irizarry

© Translated from Spanish by Joni Radcliff

and José Alejandro Peña

Published in the United States of America by
Obsidiana Press
www.obsidianapress.com
www.obsidianapress.net
www.publicatulibro.eu

E-mail

obsidianapress@gmail.com

Introduction

This, my first book on *"The Painful Harassment or School Bullying,"* is a message of love and hope for the children who suffer from such harassment or bullying.

It is also meant for parents and teachers who may share it with their children and students.

I must also mention the *"Bullies"*—that they should keep in mind not to do to others what they themselves would not like done to them, nor to their loved ones, nor to anyone at all.

In this work, the **"Stories"** are inspired by real-life events. The names, characters, and some details have been changed for creative purposes and to achieve a better narrative. Likewise, some **"Comments"** have been modified or presented as **"Anonymous."**

Acknowledgment and Dedication

First of all, I thank God for giving me life, and for granting me the necessary time to live it and share it — especially with my holy mother, now deceased, **Doña Gregoria Irizarry Laboy**, widow of Santiago, for bringing me into this world and for having given me all the love she could.

To my father, **Pedro Santiago Avilés**, also deceased, for inspiring me to write poetry, short stories, and to take an interest in Literature.

Thanks to my three children, who are my greatest inspiration and the people I love the most in life — without them, my life would have no meaning:

Gina Soto Santiago, **Jairo A. Soto Santiago**, and **Sindia I. Soto Santiago**.

To my grandchildren: **Stephanie Duprey Soto**, **Samantha R. Duprey Soto**, **Sean M. Duprey Soto**, **Tiana C. Sworn Soto**, **Kaitlyn C. Soto Pérez**, **Jordan A. Soto Santos**, and **Lyla Soto Rivera**.

Also, to my two grandchildren (not by blood) whom I love as much as the biological ones: **Matthew L. Nieves Santos** and **Isaías A. Nieves Santos**.

My great-grandchildren: *Fabian N. Acuna Duprey*, **Gabriel A. DelPolito Duprey**, **Carl A. DelPolito Duprey**,

Nicholas Johnson Duprey, Jabree Jackson Duprey, Adonis Hernández Soto, and finally, Jonah Rodríguez Soto.

Thanks to my life companion, Antonio Villegas Texidor, for his unconditional help, his patience, and understanding during the most difficult days.

To my grandchildren, who collaborated for the cover photo of this book, allowing me to take a beautiful picture as an example of survival.
They are: Melissa Batista Lozada — friend of Matthew Nieves Santos — (defender, against bullying), Jordan A. Soto Santos (center, the victim), Sean M. Duprey Soto (the bully), and Matthew Nieves Santos (defender, against bullying).

I must mention that they have nothing to do with school bullying. I invited them to pose for the cover, and with much love, they accepted.

© Cover photo: Milagros Santiago Irizarry

The Painful Harassment or School Bullying

by Milagros Santiago Irizarry

According to several experts, student harassment and bullying can be physical, emotional, verbal, through the Internet or "cyberbullying."

This so-called "Bullying" can occur in any educational institution — public school, private school, or university.

The larger the educational center, the greater the possibility of confrontations. In most cases, the lack of physical control (personal violence) and super-vision makes it more likely for these situations to occur.

There should be more staff available to supervise hallways, restrooms, the school cafeteria, and areas in front of schools — especially at dismissal time. This could help prevent vulnerable children from being chased or abused by these so-called "School Bullies."

Schools should not limit themselves only to teaching academic subjects, but should also teach about "Social Behavior."

Let us now see the difference between Harassment and School Bullying.

School Harassment:

In most cases, these are indirect or direct comments among students, using unpleasant or aggressive words with the intention to humiliate, threaten, or intimidate — with comments such as mockery, insults, inappropriate or provocative sexual remarks.

School Bullying:

This is a form of violence among classmates in which one or several students constantly and repeatedly bother or attack one or several others — both inside and outside the classroom — especially those who are more humble or unable to defend themselves effectively, and who are generally in a position of disadvantage or inferiority.

This type of bullying is prolonged and intended to intimidate and control others through physical contact, aggression, and psychological manipulation.

Harassment and Student Bullying — "Bullying" in Puerto Rico

According to the magazine Medicina y Salud Pública and the director of the Psychology Program of the Department of Education in Puerto Rico, Regina Cibes, obesity is one of the main factors that provoke "harassment and school bullying."

It is important to remember that everyone in the community shares the responsibility.

Since bullying is multifactorial, it involves teachers, mental health professionals, and parents.

For example, parents must — and should — be alert and observe their children when they return from school, keeping in mind the following warning signs:

- They appear sad or withdrawn.
- They avoid answering questions.
- They get angry easily with their siblings.
- They isolate themselves or stop communicating altogether.
- They seem constantly upset, refuse to eat, have trouble sleeping, or in the morning refuse to go to school.

It is essential to address this complex situation. Without a doubt, this is a shared responsibility — of the educational community, public schools, parents, teachers, and family members.

Parents, first and foremost, must be extremely attentive to their children, since many kids are afraid to speak about what happens to them. They avoid approaching an adult or professional at school at all costs.

Both the victim and the aggressor must be identified and interviewed separately.

Both sets of parents should be called to a meeting with those in charge of managing the situation.

The Department of Education must also offer training workshops for parents about school bullying.

After the pandemic, children's mental health has been affected by numerous problems — not only children's mental health, but societies in general — including stress, depression, anxiety, fear, uncertainty, and learning disorders among our students.

Thought and Reflection

Let us also keep in mind what often happens within the family environment.

At home, the absence of one of the parents — or sometimes the presence of a violent father or mother — can generate aggressive behavior in teenagers and even in younger children.

They learn not from what they are told to do, but from what they see around them.

Tension and poor organization in the home can also greatly contribute to aggressive behavior in many children.

Children who grow up in environments filled with violence or intimidation learn to resolve everything through violence. When they are constantly exposed to such situations, they do not develop an understanding of what empathy or compassion toward others means. They automatically record that violence in their memory, and when the opportunity arises, they express everything they have lived — using it as a tool to intimidate others, especially those who are weaker.

The weaker child may also have suffered violence, perhaps from a lack of love or attention at home, and does not know how to defend himself.

His self-esteem is very low, or nonexistent, and many of them end up taking their own lives.

These so-called "bullies" use violence and mockery as instruments of intimidation.

They believe that this behavior is correct, but they do not realize that what they are actually doing is sharing their own pain and insecurity.

These aggressors do not know how to control their impulses and emotions, nor can they distinguish between what is right and wrong.

This type of bullying destroys a child's confidence, strength, self-esteem, hope, trust, and freedom.

For that reason, parents, schools, family members, neighbors, and friends should pay closer attention and investigate whenever they notice a child who seems sad or distracted.

The child may be suffering some form of bullying and may also be under threat, afraid to speak up.

Thousands of children, in their pain, have decided to end their lives, believing there is no hope, no escape that death is the only way to be free from so much suffering.

We know that many adults are also victims of this kind of harassment, humiliation, abuse, and ridicule. It can come from their own family, their community, or even their workplace.

This undoubtedly and deeply affects their self-esteem. Out of pride or shame, they refuse to admit it.

Many end up distancing themselves from their families, moving out of their neighborhoods, and often quitting their jobs.

Let us awaken our conscience and help one another so that, together, we can help prevent this painful situation that burdens our daily lives.

"We cannot change the entire world, but united, with respect and empathy, we can make our world a better place."

It is very important to pay close attention to school bullying —not only parents, but also relatives, friends, teachers, and even the community in general.

The effects can be very serious, damaging children's sense of safety and self-esteem.

According to reports, there have been very serious cases that have led to even greater tragedies.

All of us, hand over heart, should say together:

"No to bullying, harassment, and school intimidation!"

According to Statistics

Children at Risk of Being Bullied / Risk Factors

They are often perceived as different from their classmates.

For example:

- Children who are overweight or very thin.
- Children who wear glasses or dress differently.
- Children who are new to the school, or who cannot afford the things others consider "fashionable."
- They are seen as weak or unable to defend themselves.
- They may be depressed, anxious, or have very low self-esteem.
- They are less popular than others and have few friends.
- They may not get along well with others, may be seen as annoying or provocative, or may antagonize others to attract attention.

If a child shows these risk factors, it does not necessarily mean that he or she will be bullied, but it does mean they may have a greater tendency to bully others.

In general, bullies tend to be:
- Aggressive and easily frustrated.
- Receiving little care or attention from their parents, or living in troubled homes.
- Suspicious or distrustful of others.
- Struggling to understand and respect rules.
- Viewing violence as something positive.
- Having friends who also like to bully others.

Signs and Helpful Advice to Assist Children Who Are or May Be Victims of Bullying and Harassment

For Parents
- Check your child's clothing and school bag or backpack before they leave for school.
- Then check them again when they return home.

In a discreet way, look for signs such as bruises, torn or stained clothing, or damaged school uniforms.

If they have lost a book or if some of their belongings are missing — things they had in their backpack before leaving home, such as jewelry, electronic devices, etc. — take note.

Watch for headaches or stomachaches, feelings of insecurity, or confusion.

Sometimes children pretend to be sick. We must make sure whether it is true and take the necessary steps to help them.

Changes in eating habits are also a warning sign — for

example:

"I'm not hungry."

Often, they come home hungry because they couldn't eat lunch at school — perhaps they were bullied in the cafeteria — and they don't dare to say it out of fear that their parents might investigate, making their pain even worse.

Other signs include:

- Difficulty sleeping or frequent nightmares during the night.
- Lower grades, loss of interest in schoolwork, or even refusal to go to school.
- Sudden loss of friends or refusal to participate in social events, either at home or elsewhere.
- Feelings of helplessness, believing that no one cares about them, and completely destroyed self-esteem.
- Self-destructive behavior, such as running away from home, self-harm, or talking about suicide.

Why Don't These Children Ask for Help?

School bullying creates in the child a deep sense of helplessness.

They want to handle the situation on their own, to feel in control again.

They fear being seen as weak or as "snitches."

They are afraid of retaliation from the bullies.

Bullying is, without a doubt, a humiliating and destructive experience for the most vulnerable.

They also fear being judged by adults — and possibly punished — for appearing weak.

Other Important Signs That Your Child Might Be Bullying Others:

They have friends who bully others.

They engage in physical or verbal aggression.

They are increasingly aggressive.

They are often sent to the principal's office or detention.

Sometimes they come home with more money than you gave them, or with new belongings.

They blame others for their problems.

They refuse to take responsibility for their bad actions.

They are very competitive and overly concerned with their reputation and popularity.

They believe they are "famous" for their bad behavior and enjoy the attention they receive from their peers.

Emotional Factors

Some young people who bully may themselves be or have been victims of bullying.

They may feel insecure or have very low self-esteem, and they bully others to feel more powerful.

They do not understand or recognize other people's emotions, nor do they know what respect and empathy mean.

They cannot control their own emotions, so they take revenge on others — especially the weaker ones.

It is also possible that they lack the skills to handle social situations in a healthy and positive way.

The following stories are based on real-life cases, referring to "Bullying" or student harassment and intimidation.

Story 1 — The Boy Named Nito

Nito was a victim of bullying (student harassment) by his classmates.

This went on for a long period of time.

Nito was missing one finger, and for that reason, they mocked and abused him — both physically and emotionally.

He fell into deep depression and was terrified to tell anyone, not even his parents.

In the end, he saved the life of one of his tormentors — one of the boys who used to bully him — from being run over by a cargo truck, teaching him a life-changing lesson.

Especially for parents, this story reminds us to watch and ask where our children are, what they're doing, and who their friends are.

It's also important to communicate with their teachers and find out how they behave in class.

Characters
1. Nito – The victim; shy and kind.
2. Moni – Leader of the bullying group; aggressive and cruel.
3. Laica – Nito's mother; very worried about her son.

4. Motilio – Nito's father; also concerned.
5. Doña Dora – Teacher and principal of the school, and Moni's mother.

Middle School: "Los VIP"
Grade: Sixth
Time: 8:30 a.m.
Students: 12

First Scene

In the classroom, before lunchtime.

Moni: "Look at him!" (turning to his friends) "He thinks he's so great — missing a finger!"
(He laughs, and all his friends join in.)

Nito knew they were talking about him. Filled with anguish, he ran out of the classroom straight home. Everyone else went silent.

Doña Dora was writing an assignment on the board. Then she turned around, and seeing that Nito wasn't there, asked:

Doña Dora: "What happened to Nito? He left the classroom without permission!"

Bullies: "No, teacher... we don't know." (They looked at each other, many of them smirking.)

The teacher ignored the incident and continued the lesson without informing Nito's parents.

At Nito's Home

Nito arrived home very early, threw his backpack on the

floor, and locked himself in his room.

Laica (his mother) knocked on the door:

"What happened, son? You're home so early!"

Nito (without opening the door):

"I just had a stomachache, so I left."

Laica (thinking):

"That's strange... they haven't called me from the school."

"Come eat, son."

She tried to open the door — he resisted, but as a mother, she used her authority and managed to get in. She sat on the bed next to him, held his hands tenderly, and asked:

Laica: "What happened, son? Why didn't you tell your teacher?"

Nito: "I didn't want to interrupt, Mom."

Laica (worried):

"I'll have to go to the school and see what's going on." (She ended up forgetting to go or call.)

Laica: "Son, if you keep this up, I'll call your doctor. And when your father gets home, we'll go see the doctor."

Nito: "No, Mom, I'll be fine." (He looked anxious.)

Laica: "Alright, my son. Let's see how you feel — but if it continues, we'll go to the doctor whether you like it or not."

Nito made faces and went to sleep.

Later, his father came home.

Motilio: "Did Nito eat?"

Laica: "No, he didn't. He went to bed early. Said he wasn't feeling well."
Motilio: "What's wrong?"
Laica: "He said his stomach hurts, but not much."
Motilio: "Well, we'll keep an eye on him in case we need to take him to the doctor."

The Next Day

Seeing her son's mood, Nito's mother decided to walk him to school every morning — just three blocks from their home.

Nito didn't want to, but she insisted, using her motherly authority, and he had to agree.

In the Classroom

Nito arrived at school with his mother, still afraid.

He went to class a few minutes early.

Meanwhile, Moni and two other bullies were whispering in the hallway, planning how they would torment Nito that day.

Class began, and Nito started feeling sick.

Nito: "Teacher, may I go to the bathroom?"

Doña Dora: "Yes, you may." (He left.)

A couple of minutes later—

Moni: "Teacher, can I go to the bathroom? It's an emergency."

(He held his stomach, pretending it was real.)

Doña Dora: "Alright, go."

He left, followed secretly by the other bullies.

Outside the bathroom, Moni and his gang waited for Nito to come out.

When he did, trembling—

Moni: "Hey, you! Where was that finger when you cut it off?"

(Laughter.)

"Did you clean yourself properly with only the four you have left?"

(More laughter.)

They ran back to class before Nito returned.

Nito entered the room, shaking. The teacher kept writing on the board, unaware of what had happened.

Class ended.

Nito ran home without waiting for anyone.

Laica: "What happened, son? You're early again!"

Nito: "No, Mom — I just ran to get here before you, so you wouldn't have to walk again."

Laica: "Don't do that, son. I'm not working right now, so wait for me next time."

Nito: "Okay, Mom." (Hiding his pain.)

He sat down to eat dinner with his parents, pretending everything was fine.

Laica: "How was school today, son?"

Motilio: "Yes, tell us!"

Nito: "It was great, Mom."

Laica: "Do you have homework?"

Nito: "No, not today."

He went to his room, watched a bit of TV, took a shower, and went to bed.

Fourth Scene

The next morning, Nito woke up with fever and diarrhea.

His parents took him to the doctor, who prescribed medicine.

He stayed in bed all day and slept better that night.

The following day, he returned to school.

Scene: 8:30 a.m., School Hallway

Moni: "Let's see how we can bother Nito today."

(Laughter.)

All his friends agreed and went to class.

Moni: "Boring. We couldn't bother Nito today."

The Next Day

When Nito arrived at school, he saw Moni and his gang beating up two students.

He gathered his courage and shouted:

Nito: "What are you doing? Stop it, you idiots!"

Moni: "I'll kill you if you say anything!"

The other bullies ran away.

Moni tried to cross the street to attack Nito —without looking— just as a large truck was speeding by.

Nito ran into the street, risking his own life, and shouted to the driver:

Nito: "Watch out!"

The driver slammed on the brakes, terrified.

Moni barely escaped being hit.

The truck drove away.

Moni, trembling and crying, turned to Nito.

Moni: "You saved my life! Why?"

Nito (calm but firm): "Yes. Even though you've hurt me for a long time, I have no wish to harm you.

I think now you are the one who needs more help than I do."

He gently placed his thumb on Moni's forehead and said:

"And let me tell you something..."

Then, lowering his voice, still pressing his thumb against Moni's forehead, added:

"Next time you try to bully me, I swear I'll defend myself."

Moni, deeply ashamed, replied:

"Forgive me, Nito."

He hugged him tightly.

Moni: "I promise I'll never bother you or anyone else again."

They walked back to school together, joined by Moni's friends — who also apologized to Nito.

When they arrived, late for class, Doña Dora looked at them and said:

"What's going on? Why are you so late?"

Moni: "Forgive me, Mom!"

Everyone was stunned — no one knew that the teacher was Moni's mother.

She had always left home earlier than him, so no one ever suspected.

Nito: "Your mom? You never told us!"

Moni: "She asked me not to."

Then, turning to his mother, Moni said:

"Forgive me, Mom. I was the bully at school... but I'm truly sorry.

Nito taught me a lesson and saved me from being crushed under a truck."

Nito: "It's true, ma'am."

Doña Dora, deeply moved, apologized to Nito and said to her son:

"Forgive me, son, for not being more careful with you.

At home, you'll lose most of your privileges so you can learn your lesson and learn to respect others."

She went to her office and suspended him for two weeks.

A meeting was held with parents and teachers to discuss ways to better support their children and students. They agreed to put up a sign at the school entrance that read: "Free of Harassment or Bullying."

Moral

Don't do to anyone what you wouldn't want done to you or to someone you love.

Think before you speak or hurt others.
Not everything you hear or think is true.

Life is full of surprises, and when you least expect it, you might find yourself needing help from the very person you once hurt.

Story 2 — The Black Girl

Originally from Africa, her name was Nachi.
(Story collaboration by Adán Santiago Irizarry — Middle School Teacher.)
A family member brought her from Africa to the United States, where her parents lived.

Nachi's parents were very busy people, always struggling to survive in a world full of so many needs —and above all, in a society filled with discrimination, where human mistreatment seems to have no limits.
People are often despised or abused simply for being different— whether by race, gender, political beliefs, religion, or poverty, among other things.
By nature, we are all unique and different in every sense. If we consider ourselves truly educated — not just by titles or formal recognition, but by knowing how to handle, understand, and work with humanity through respect and empathy — then our world could become a better world.
In Nachi's case, her parents' daily responsibilities kept them from noticing how lonely and abandoned their daughter felt.
When she entered middle school, her mental and emo-

tional agony began, because she was the only black student in her class.

Nachi felt rejected by everyone.

No one wanted to talk to her.

Whenever she tried to approach one of her classmates, they would move away and make faces of disgust.

This filled her with fear, and she walked the school hallways confused and afraid.

She didn't dare complain to anyone, fearing retaliation.

One day, terrified to enter her classroom, she hid behind a telephone booth near the school's entrance.

As students and staff walked by, many looked at her with disdain — simply because she was a Black student. She almost dragged her feet as she walked, and when she was finally discovered, she went through a painful and heartbreaking experience — but in the end, she found the strength to forgive and even make good friends, despite the harm she had suffered.

Characters

1. Nachi – The victim; the Black girl.
2. Gigi – A gentle, kind girl.
3. Diego – A boy who was also bullied because of his weight; he didn't care much, laughed it off, and often chased the bullies down the hall.
4. Mateo – A bully, but one capable of empathy.
5. Mauro – A bully; mocked and laughed at everyone.
6. Javier – Kind.

7. Bruno – Kind and empathetic.
8. Pablo – A bully.

First Scene

Setting: In front of the school.
A cold, windy morning.

Nachi walked anxiously and nervously, but determined to enter her school.

She asked herself:

"Will there be anyone near me who doesn't care that I'm a Black student? Hmm... it doesn't seem like it."

Seeing Nachi so nervous, Gigi approached her and said:

"Hi, what's wrong? Why are you so nervous?"

Nachi didn't answer.

She froze, terrified at being noticed by the other students — many of whom were bullies.

Suddenly, Mauro and Pablo lunged toward her, shouting: "Ebola! Ebola!"

They compared her to a contagious disease — an unpleasant, infectious virus — and yelled:

"Go away! You're Black, you stink, and you're ugly! You'll bring us bad luck! We don't want you near us!"

Nachi: "No! Leave me alone! I just want to go to my classroom!"

Then Mateo noticed the attack.

He was usually one of those who laughed at others when he didn't like them — but in that moment, he felt deep empathy.

He ran and threw himself between them, shouting:

"WHAT ARE YOU DOING? LEAVE HER ALONE! DON'T BE CRUEL! ARE YOU DISCRIMINATING JUST BECAUSE SHE'S BLACK?"

He kept shouting furiously:

"COLOR DOESN'T MATTER! WE ARE ALL HUMAN BEINGS, AND WE DESERVE RESPECT AND EMPATHY TOWARD ONE ANOTHER!"

He continued speaking loudly for everyone to hear:

"MANY TIMES, IN OUR LIVES, WE COME ACROSS UNGRATEFUL PEOPLE WHO DON'T KNOW HOW TO TREAT OTHERS, WHO PLANT FEAR AND INSECURITY IN THEM — AND THAT CAN DAMAGE US FOR THE REST OF OUR LIVES."

Mateo went on, filled with sadness and regret for having been a bully himself in the past:

"Today, in front of all of you, I proudly say NO TO BULLYING — student and nonstudent harassment alike.

From now on, I'll be watching closely for any bullies in our school.

I'll teach them a life lesson — about empathy, kindness, and respect for others."

Everyone lowered their heads in silence.

Those who had been bullies felt ashamed and remorseful.

Moved by Mateo's words, they experienced a wave of mixed emotions — but through it, they learned a powerful lesson of love and respect for others, no matter

where they come from or what ethnic group they belong to.

They ended up singing together a song called "Forgive
me", filled with joy and unity.

Then Diego appeared, pretending not to care, sat near
them — and eventually joined in singing with the group.
By the end, Nachi was accepted by everyone, overcom-
ing her fears and insecurities about being black.

Story 3 — The Autistic Girl

A story about the courage of one mother teaching her son about the pain and consequences of hurting others — and the carelessness of another mother, who could have prevented her special, autistic daughter's suffering.

This autistic girl, named Sophie, loved to climb trees. That simple activity made her feel calm and relaxed. Sometimes she climbed with her mother beside her, who watched over her lovingly and patiently; other times, she liked to do it on her own.

One day, while her mother was busy talking on the phone, Sophie quietly slipped away.
She wanted to walk to school by herself and do all the mischievous things she loved — like climbing her favorite tree, and then walking alone to her nearby school.
When her mother realized she was gone, she began to worry.

Then she thought, "She's probably already at school."
(It wasn't the first time Sophie had done this.)
Still, she called the school — and they confirmed that Sophie had arrived safely to her classroom.

Characters

1. Sophie – The autistic girl (the victim). Sometimes calm, sometimes aggressive.
2. Tricia – Sophie's mother (a single mother).
3. Rodrigo – The bully; aggressive and mocking.
4. Bambi – Rodrigo's sister.
5. Tatiana – Mother of Rodrigo and Bambi (deeply concerned about her son's behavior).
6. Mrs. Inés – The school principal; active and alert.

Scene: *The road to school*
A tree-lined path on both sides.

Tatiana walks with her two children, Rodrigo and Bambi, on their way to school.

Suddenly, they see Sophie trying to climb her favorite tree.

Rodrigo: "Look, Mom! That crazy girl! She's such an idiot — trying to climb a tree! What's wrong with her?" (he laughs cruelly)

"I want to push her so she falls and breaks her bones for being so dumb!"

Tatiana grabs him by the arm and says:

"Don't you dare! I know that girl — she's autistic, very sweet and very special. She could even be your friend. Remember, you have a little sister who's also special. Don't forget that, understand?"

She continued:

"Her mother, Ms. Tricia, usually walks her to school. I

don't know what happened today."

(It was the first time they happened to take the same path that Sophie and her mother used to reach school.) Rodrigo rolled his eyes and grumbled, pretending to agree with his mother, while his sister Bambi stayed very quiet.

Sophie ran off and reached the school before them.

Tatiana dropped off her kids and returned home.

In the school hallway, Rodrigo saw Sophie walking toward the special education classroom — the same one his sister Bambi attended.

Smirking, he thought:

"Hmm... I have to do something to mess with her."

Later that day, classes ended, and Rodrigo and Bambi had to walk home alone.

Rodrigo planned to bother Sophie on her way home, but as he was waiting, he saw Sophie's mother arrive to pick her up.

Rodrigo: "Ugh, how annoying — she's getting picked up today!"

Tricia: "Sweetie, don't walk to school alone again like you did yesterday. Always wait for me. I called the school and they told me you got there fine."

Sophie: "But Mom! You were too busy talking on the phone!"

Tricia: "Even so, you should've waited for me."

Sophie: "Okay, Mom." (She didn't tell her about the scare she had that day, when Rodrigo tried to attack her.)

That day, Rodrigo's mother couldn't pick up her children, so Rodrigo walked home with Bambi.

Once home, he locked himself in his room to make a phone call.

Tatiana: "What's he planning now?" (She approached his door and overheard him plotting to harass Sophie.)

Tatiana: "This can't be... my son? No. Absolutely not."

That night after dinner, everyone went to bed — but Tatiana couldn't sleep.

She thought:

"I have to teach my son a lesson — one about respect and empathy."

The next morning — at the family breakfast table

Tatiana: "Rodrigo, you and your sister will have to walk to school alone today. I can't go with you. Take care of her, okay?"

Rodrigo, with a sly and satisfied grin:

"Sure, Mom. Of course."

As soon as they left, Tatiana picked up the phone and called the school office.

Tatiana: "Good morning! May I speak with Mrs. Inés, please?"

Mrs. Inés: "Good morning! Speaking. How can I help you?"

Tatiana: "Good morning. This is Rodrigo's mother. I'm

very sad to have to call about this, but I want to teach my son a lesson — a lesson in respect and empathy toward others."

Mrs. Inés: "Yes, of course, Mrs. Tatiana. What's going on?"

Tatiana: "Last night, I overheard my son saying on the phone that he planned to bother Sophie, the autistic girl, when she got to school today.

I sent him early this morning so I could arrive before them and prevent anything from happening.

I think someone else might be involved too, but I couldn't hear everything."

Mrs. Inés stood up, shocked.

"What should we do?"

Tatiana: "I'll get there before they do. I'll hide behind that big tree by the school courtyard — the one near the entrance. Please meet me there without letting anyone notice."

Mrs. Inés (astonished): "Yes, yes — I'll be there, Mrs. Tatiana. This can't happen at my school. My God..."

Scene: *In front of the school courtyard — 8:00 AM*
A beautiful tree decorates the front area.

Mrs. Inés, the principal, hides cautiously behind the tree. Soon after, Mrs. Tatiana arrives.

They meet, as planned, and quietly wait to see if Rodrigo will actually do what he'd said the night before.

Bambi, Rodrigo's sister, who was also autistic, wore her

hair the same way as Sophie — in a ponytail — and both wore the same uniform.

Of course, they attended the same school.

As the two girls walked toward the entrance — first Bambi, then Sophie — Rodrigo and his friends jumped out and attacked the girl they thought was Sophie.

But they had attacked the wrong girl.

They had beaten Bambi, Rodrigo's own sister.

Mrs. Inés and Mrs. Tatiana ran to help her, but it was too late.

They had no choice but to call the authorities.

Rodrigo, the ringleader, was taken away by the police.

The others involved were also suspended from school.

After several hours in custody, their parents picked them up, and the boys were grounded for a week — no friends, no phone calls, no privileges.

It was a harsh lesson.

Two weeks later, tragedy struck.

Rodrigo's mother, Tatiana, passed away.

Rodrigo and Bambi were left heartbroken — and were eventually adopted.

In her honor, Rodrigo gathered his old friends — some of them former bullies now filled with remorse.

He invited Sophie, Bambi, Diego, Pablo, and Gigi to meet in the Hummingbird Forest, a place where they used to race and play together.

They also looked for Mateo, Mauro, Bruno, and Javier.

Most of them had also been adopted by a loving couple, Edam and Lisandra, who had a big house and dedicated their lives to adopting children from shelters, orphanages, or kids who had run away from home.

As it happened, the adopted children had run away again for a few days.

The reunion was full of laughter and jokes.

After a while, Rodrigo stepped away, deep in thought — then returned with a new idea.

Rodrigo:

"Everyone, can I have your attention, please?"

He stood proudly and said:

"In honor of my mother, Tatiana — who gave everything for us, who loved us even when we weren't her own children, who taught us to care for one another — I want to say this:

She always told us that people who adopt can become true friends, that we should seek out love and kindness in them.

I made mistakes. I got into trouble. I was adopted. I ran away.

But now I want to go back."

He smiled and added:

"Before we go back, let's ask others what they think about this thing called bullying."

Then, filled with joy, he looked around at his friends and said: "Shall we go home?"

They all shouted together: "Yeeees!"

Sophie and Bambi:

"It's been a while since we've been home. Our adoptive parents must be so worried! But before we go back, let's stop by that beautiful house we saw the other day." (It was actually their adoptive parents' home — but it looked so different after being remodeled that they didn't recognize it.)

Sophie:

"Let's see who answers the door. Maybe our adoptive parents don't want us back — and if that's true, maybe these people will adopt us."

Everyone: "Yeeees!"

Back Home

Characters
Children (Adopted):
1. Rodrigo – Adopted, former bully.
2. Sophie – The autistic girl (adopted).
3. Bambi – Rodrigo's adopted sister.
4. Diego – Adopted.
5. Pablo – Adopted.
6. Mateo – Adopted.
7. Mauro – Adopted.
8. Bruno – Adopted.
9. Javier – Adopted.

Adoptive Parents:
1. Lisandra
2. Edam

Rodrigo knocked on the door insistently.

After a moment, a woman appeared —Mrs. Lisandra, holding a rolled-up wet towel, ready to swing it at who-ever it was.

But when she saw them...

"Whaaaat!!"

Everyone froze in place.

"That's our adoptive mother!!"

All of them gathered together in silence and respect.

Mrs. Lisandra, still shocked, called out:

"Edam! Come here! Look who's back— the rascals! The ungrateful ones who left us for so long!

And look — they're not even alone, they've brought company!"

Edam: "A bunch of ungrateful kids! We were about to report your disappearance. We've been waiting for you. Come in — we have a lot to talk about."

The children, nervous and ashamed, went up the steps slowly.

Rodrigo stepped forward and apologized for everyone.

Then they began explaining all the problems they had gone through — how some of them had become bullies and had run away from home.

Edam:

"We suffered a lot because of your absence.

We didn't report you right away — we thought maybe you'd gone back to the places you came from, and we didn't want you punished.

But we were just about to make the report."

He continued:

"That's why we made some changes to the front of the house — to mislead you, in case you ever decided to come back.

But look at you — you fell right into our trap and returned to your own home without realizing it!"

Everyone burst into nervous laughter.

Edam:

"We wanted you to learn a lesson — to be kind, and to respect one another, even if you think you already know everything.

We'll keep teaching you how to love and respect each other."

Then he looked straight at the ones who had once been bullies.

They looked at each other, eyes down, ashamed.

Edam: "Are you hungry?"

Everyone: "Yeees!"

Lisandra: "Then first — showers, all of you!"

They all glanced at each other, and she continued,

"One at a time, in order — take turns!"

A few days later, their adoptive parents, Edam and Lisandra, woke up full of joy.

They were so happy to see that their adopted children were finally behaving well — that they had truly learned about love, respect, and empathy toward others.

That morning, they made an announcement:

"We're going to have a party to celebrate your progress!"

All the children jumped up, cheering with excitement.

Collaborators:

Adán Santiago Irizarry – Elementary School Teacher, brother of the author.

Firefighter Jairo A. Soto Santiago – Son of the author and father of Jordan.

Comments: June 20, 2017

- **Boy, 11 years old** (Name withheld)
1. "I think bullying is wrong, but sometimes bullies have something wrong in their minds and they don't realize that they're suffering too."
- **Girl, 5 years old** (Name withheld)
2. "Bullying, to me, is when someone pushes me, tries to bite me, says bad things about me, makes mean jokes, or sometimes doesn't let me play with the toys at daycare or in my doctor's office."
- **Single Mother, 34 years old** (Name withheld)

"Bullying" is a very sensitive topic to talk about —at least, for me it is.

I've been bullied for as long as I can remember.

The earliest I can trace it back is to my elementary school days.

I was very young, just like my two siblings —a brother and a sister— I'm the oldest of the three.

We moved to another town, and changing schools made me very afraid.

On my first day, I arrived terrified. Being the new student, in first grade, I felt like I didn't belong — not in that school, not even in that classroom.

No one wanted to be my friend.

I felt lonely and sad, and the only thing I could do was

follow whatever my teachers told me.

I remember feeling sad and alone all the time — all I wanted was for someone to talk to me.

That year just went by, and nothing changed.

The next year, I entered second grade.

I'll never forget the time I got into trouble for defending myself against a bully.

I kept crying — I couldn't understand what was happening to me.

I'm grateful for that day, though, because I met someone very important.

It was a teacher — everyone respected him and liked him.

He helped many students who struggled with learning difficulties.

He was unique in every sense.

He helped me overcome the bullying all the way through fifth grade.

He used to call me his "little tiger."

Unfortunately, he couldn't save me once I entered middle school or high school.

My mental and emotional health got worse over time.

When I started middle school, I became the "teacher's pet."

Other kids hated the way teachers praised me.

They shoved me into lockers, pushed me down the stairs, called me horrible names.

They started rumors about me.
Some kids even pretended to be my friends — just so they could make fun of me more.
My childhood innocence began to fade.
My spirit started to break.
I began to feel like a lost little girl.
And I had no idea that high school would be even worse.
I was always a depressed and anxious child.
So, you can probably guess what I was like as a teenager — painfully shy.
I only made a few friends because of it.
What I went through in high school made my depression worse.
Those experiences made me want to run away — made me feel like ending my life.
I kept feeling like there was no way out of this hellish world.
You're probably wondering what I'm like now, as an adult.
Well, let's just say that if it weren't for my four beautiful children, I wouldn't be here today.
I fight my emotional and mental demons every single day — only for them.
They give me the strength to live.
They show me what real love is.
Don't worry about me — I'll be okay.
I will keep fighting.
Now, I'll end my story with this:

If you're bullying someone, remember this — words can hurt just as much as hitting someone.

Please, stop — and think about that person.

You will end up being responsible for their life.

And if you are being bullied — listen to my words:

There is a way out.

Fight back, run, tell someone — someone who will listen and help you.

Bullies are not worth your life.

The End

December 12, 2023

About the Author

Her name is Milagros Santiago Irizarry.

She is Puerto Rican and currently resides in the state of New Jersey, United States.

She was born in a humble neighborhood called "El Saltillo," in Adjuntas, Puerto Rico.

She traveled to the United States around the middle of 1968 in search of a better future — not only for herself, but also for her mother and siblings — something that still fills her with great satisfaction.

She is the mother of three wonderful children — one son and two daughters — and now enjoys the great blessing of being both a grandmother and great-grandmother.

After 21 years of marriage, she divorced due to "incompatibility of character."

In the U.S., she pursued higher education at Essex County College in Newark, New Jersey, as well as at Rutgers University and Berkeley College (NJ), earning a degree in Psychology and Social Work.

She is now enjoying her well-deserved retirement.

Her last position was at the Superior Court of New Jersey, where she worked for 19 years as a Child Support Investigator and Probation Officer within the same department.

She has always been passionate about creative writing, poetry, and all other forms of artistic or communicative expression.

Her first published book was a bilingual poetry collection titled: "Poemas Y Más... Pensando En Ti Mamá" ("Poems and More... Thinking of You, Mom"), officiallly released in May 2013.

She has participated in numerous literary and cultural festivals, poetry contests, and narrative gatherings, such as:

1. **Latin American Association of Culture (A.L.A.C.), Paterson, NJ — Honorable Mention**

• *Quién será mamá* (2004)

• *Aquí estoy papá* — Second Prize in Poetry, 2005

2. **Festival of the Latin American Song of Culture, California (2009) — Diploma of Excellence**

• *Cuando los hijos se van*

3. "Festí Vegas Internacional" (2009) — Diplomas of Excellence

- *Con los ángeles del cielo*
- *Pensando en ti mamá*
- *Ámame pacientemente* — dedicated to special children, including those with autism and other conditions.

In December 2023, she wrote a heartfelt song titled ***"Perdónenme"*** ("Forgive Me"), in which bullies ask forgiveness from their victims.

It is dedicated to children who suffer from harassment and school bullying ("bullying") at the hands of others.

Forgive Me

We are no longer those kids
Who made you feel small and alone,
We want to be friends again
In search of a better world.
We'll always keep a space
Right here in our hearts,
To share with tenderness
Love, respect, and care.
We'll be brothers of the soul
And we want to ask your pardon —
Forgive us, a thousand times forgive us!
Our hearts overflow

With love and sorrow combined.
No one ever knew the story
That made us behave so wrong,
But today we stand before you all,
Look deep into our eyes —
You will see the pain and sadness
That will fade forevermore
If only you grant us your forgiveness.

She also loves the theater, having performed in the "Teatro Valentín" in New Jersey, where she participated in several stage productions.
Milagros remains the same kindhearted person she has always been —full of empathy, humility, respect, and genuine consideration for others.

Table of Content

This first edition of
The Painful Harassment or School Bullying,

by Milagros Santiago Irizarry, was completed in print

in October 2025.

Published in the United States of America by
Obsidiana Press

www.obsidianapress.com

www.obsidianapress.net

www.publicatulibro.eu

E-Mail:

obsidianapress@gmail.com

www.ingramcontent.com/pod-product-compliance
Lightning Source LLC
Chambersburg PA
CBHW032217040426
42449CB00005B/641